Don't Tease Mr. Beeze

Written by Shawn Thorn
Illustrated by Shawn Thorn
& Johnny

Library of Congress Cataloging-in-Publication Data
Thorn, Shawn
Don't Tease Mr. Beeze / Written and Illustrated by Shawn Thorn
Illustrated by Johnny
Editor: Vincenzo Coia
p. cm.
Summary: Illustrations and rhyming text portray children
experiencing a range of emotions, including: teasing, bullying,
geography, fear, excitement, happiness, kindness
ISBN 78-0-9940979
Illustrations rendered in pastel pencil and Photoshop
Text set in Noteworthy Light

Instagram: shawn.thorn
Website: shawnthornbooks.com

Hi, have you ever teased a bee? Well, I have, and it wasn't very smart, you'll see.

Yep, you'll see!

I shouldn't have done what I did, but I did, and it all started soon after I turned five.

And in my backyard, I taunted, pestered and teased a hive.

I knew teasing was wrong, my mother told me all along.

I don't know why I wouldn't listen; my dad said, "Son, you'll learn your lesson!"

So, again I teased,
and he pointed
to his stinger and
said, "No more, you'll
be sore!"

And then the chase began! He chased me on my feet.

I ran faster
and the bee
flew swifter, as he
chased me up my street.

He also
chased me to
Costa Blanca
on a rock
climbing hike.

And he chased me
through Yellowstone
National Park
on a bike.

He chased me
through a country
farm in Switzerland,
on a goat.

Then he chased
me through
the Italian
Riviera

on a boat.

He chased me to New York City, through Central Park, and over a fountain.

That bee even chased me snowboarding to the top of Whistler Mountain.

He even chased
me 384,400
kilometers
to the moon.

It wasn't until we ran by Vancouver's steam clock that I knew it was noon.

He sent me a text and even called me on the phone.

And he chased me all the way back to my home.

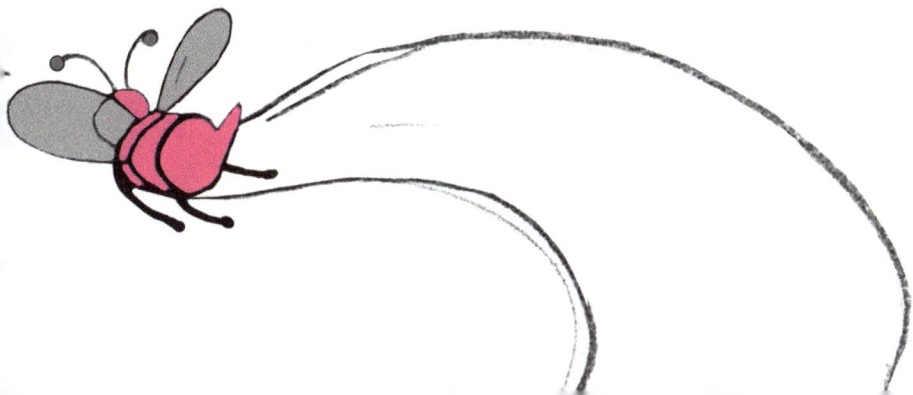

From North America to the moon, and Spain over to Italy, from Canada to the U.S.A., and from here to there and everywhere, he chased me with great fear!

Then it happened! Without a doubt, he stung me on my rear!

He said, "I didn't want to sting you, but when we are being teased, this is what we do."

He stuck out his
thumb and said,
"Even friendly me,
Mr. Beeze."

To all the children that have inspired me to teach, mentor and learn.
I would like to espcially thank all my nieces and nephews:
Tamara, Emmotions, Shawna, Jasmine, Destiny, Jenee,
Michaela, Keni and Milaana, Christopher and Tone Romone.
I work with kids today because of you all.
I would like to thank some of the special children who I have
taught and mentored over the years, such as Amira, Adrian, Jonathan,
Bryan, Joben, Shaan, Smira, Rikki, Noor, Jack,
Tyler, Alex, Kyle, Jason, Norman and dozens more.
Audrey, "I love you a hundred, a thousand, a million, a billion; I love you a trillion."
Frankie and Freddie, my twin Godsons, and to Jacob, my sorta Godson, and to Sierra, Kayden & baby Green;
to Hayden and Morgan, my cousins who I think of often, but don't see often enough.
You all bring me a perfect happiness each time I am with you, and each time I think of you.

and lastly, my mother.

I practice kindness because of you. I aspire because of you. I love because of you.

Thank you!

www.ingramcontent.com/pod-product-compliance
Lightning Source LLC
Chambersburg PA
CBHW062007090426
42811CB00005B/774